CROWNED HEART SERIES — BOOK TWO

Clara Dunn

Written by Melanie Lotfali
Illustrated by Katayoun Mottahedin

The Crowned Heart Series – Clara Dunn

Text © Melanie Lotfali
Illustrations © Katayoun Mottahedin
Original book design by Monib Mahdavi

First Edition 2008
Second Edition 2016
All Rights Reserved

Licensed under a Creative Commons
Attribution-NonCommercial-ShareAlike 4.0
International License

hardcover ISBN 978-0-99456018-1-0
softcover ISBN 978-0-9945926-7-5

How many queens of the world have laid down their heads on a pillow of dust and disappeared... Not so the handmaids who ministered at the Threshold of God; these have shone forth like glittering stars in the skies of ancient glory, shedding their splendors across all the reaches of time.

'Abdu'l-Bahá

There are queens who wear crowns on their heads. Their crowns are made of earthly things like gold and diamonds and rubies.

And there are queens who wear crowns in their hearts. Their crowns are made of heavenly things, like love and courage and humility. This is the story about one of those queens. Her name is Clara Dunn.

Clara Dunn lived in America. When 'Abdu'l-Bahá visited America she travelled a long way to meet him. 'Abdu'l-Bahá taught Clara Dunn about truthfulness.

Abdu'l-Bahá wrote letters to His Bahá'í friends, asking for their help. Just like Martha Root, Clara Dunn wanted to be His helper.

So Clara and her husband, Hyde Dunn, sailed to Australia.

Clara and Hyde Dunn were the very first Bahá'ís to go to Australia. They lived in lots of different cities.

Everyone who came to Clara Dunn's home was welcome. She loved all people.

Clara Dunn hosted special meetings at her home, called firesides. She made delicious food and invited people to come for dinner.

Then Hyde Dunn talked about Bahá'u'lláh and His Teachings. After his talk Clara and Hyde Dunn answered questions while the stars came out at night.

Sometimes the meetings went very late. People didn't want to leave Clara and Hyde Dunn's house. But they didn't mind, they loved hosting firesides.

Many Australians learned about Bahá'u'lláh through Clara Dunn and her firesides. For the new Bahá'ís Clara was their spiritual mother. So they called her Mother Dunn.

Mother Dunn was truly a spiritual queen. The crown in her heart shone with the sparkling gem of loving kindness.

Hand of the Cause of God
Clara Dunn

REFERENCES

The stories and facts contained in this book are from:
Harper, Barron. *"Lights of Fortitude"*. August, 1997. George Ronald, Oxford, Great Britain.

Melanie Lotfali

Melanie Lotfali PhD is a graduate of the Australian College of Journalism in Professional Writing for Children. She is the author of the Fellowship Farm series, Unity in Diversity series, and Crowned Heart series.

She currently lives in Townsville, Australia, with her family.

Katayoun Mottahedin

Katayoun Mottahedin has a Post Graduate Diploma of Education from Monash University, Bachelor of Graphic Design from Swinburne University of Technology and Diploma of Arts and Design from Chisholm Institute. Her art has been utilised in magazines, books, greeting cards, stationary and other publications.

She currently lives in Melbourne, Australia.